D0971297

The Book of

Murray

Also by David M. Bader

Haikus for Jews: For You, a Little Wisdom

Zen Judaism: For You, a Little Enlightenment

The **Book** of

Murray

———◆◆———

THE LIFE, TEACHINGS, AND KVETCHING OF THE LOST PROPHET

———◆◆———

Edited with an Introduction by

David M. Bader

Harmony Books / New York

Copyright © 2010 by David M. Bader

Published in the United States by Harmony Books,
an imprint of the Crown Publishing Group,
a division of Random House, Inc., New York.
www.crownpublishing.com

Harmony Books is a registered trademark and the Harmony
Books colophon is a trademark of Random House, Inc.

Library of Congress Cataloging-in-Publication Data is
available upon request.

ISBN 978-0-307-45324-2

Printed in the United States of America

10   9   8   7   6   5   4   3   2   1

First Edition

contents

Contents

The Book of

Murray

introduction

In the modern world, the lives and teachings of
biblical prophets often seem remote and dim in
our consciousness. And of all these narratives,
The Book of Murray may well be the dimmest.
This little-known work, a relatively recent addi-
tion to the religious canon, has baffled biblical
scholars since its discovery. Still, it is assigned
reading at some universities and seminaries,
possibly because it is very difficult to get anyone
to read it voluntarily.

The saga of how *The Book of Murray* first
came to light begins in the land of Israel in ancient times. It resumes centuries later in Boca
Raton, Florida, on the 14th hole of the golf
course at Kibbitzing Pines Country Club. There,

on either his third or fifteenth attempt to chip out of a sand trap (accounts vary), retired hosiery importer Leo Plotnick struck something hard and hollow.

When he investigated, he was surprised to discover a buried earthenware vessel. Inside it were scrolls of parchment, untouched and unread for thousands of years, filled with sacred writings painstakingly inscribed with a primitive stylus, all covered with some sort of mold that was murder on his sinuses. Among these scrolls, now known as the Boca Scrolls, was one bearing the title *The Book of Murray*.

Experts who examined *The Book of Murray* immediately questioned its authenticity. How had scrolls purporting to be from biblical times made their way to Florida? Why were they so different in both tone and appearance from other ancient scrolls? Most importantly, why was there no mention of anyone named Murray in other biblical texts? The result was a schism among biblical scholars so great that a number of them called for the manuscript to be taken back to the golf course and reburied in an even deeper hole.

The historical significance of *The Book of Murray* began to emerge only when carbon dating showed that the scrolls were indeed quite old. Soon after, stains on the parchment—confirmed to contain trace amounts of brisket—were removed to reveal the complete text. For years, scholars had been puzzling over the stark contrasts between modern Judaism and the world of the Israelites of the Torah, the Prophets, and the Writings. Leviticus might contain guidance on keeping kosher, but where was the scriptural support for pocketing a dinner roll from a buffet "for later"? In *The Book of Murray*, scholars finally found answers. Here was the missing link that showed that today's Jews and their ancestors had more in common than previously seemed imaginable.

And yet, *The Book of Murray* continues to raise as many questions as it answers. Who was Murray? Will his teachings add significantly to our understanding of important religious principles? And why was his book buried where it was?*

Prophetic words spoken in one age are not always entirely intelligible in another. This is especially the case when, as with *The Book of Murray*, they were not entirely intelligible the first time around. For all its difficulties, though, *The Book of Murray* offers a unique perspective on the distant past that explains much about the present. Three thousand years after it was written, Murray's age-old yet oddly contemporary wisdom still teaches us much about ourselves.

The prophets of ancient Israel—men such

---

*To save time, the answers are, in order, "Who knows?" "Highly unlikely," and "Because."

as Amos, Isaiah, and Jeremiah—while divinely inspired, were deeply involved in the world around them. So too was Murray. The pages that follow remind us that these men of God were very much students of the human condition. They also remind us that some of them were better students than others.

David M. Bader
August 2010

chapter 1

The Birth of the Prophet

And it came to pass that the descendants of Abraham and Isaac and Jacob went into Canaan, for they sought water and pasture for their flocks. And it was a place of peaceable hills and valleys, with rains that came in due season, low crime, low taxes, and a goodly public school system. Verily, it was a land flowing with milk and honey.

And they were called the Tribe of Levi (Relaxed Fit) and these were their generations: Jedidiah begat Zedidiah, and Zedidiah begat Zebediah, and Zebediah begat Obadiah, and Obadiah begat Irving. And Irving took unto him a wife, Francine, and they were called the Silvermans. But they were without child and begat no one.

And the Silvermans prayed and beseeched the Lord to open Francine's womb, yet her womb remained closed. And they made burnt offerings of rams and heifers and loaves of barley to the Lord, but it availed them not. And they offered coffee rings and bagels and whitefish salad to the Lord, yet she did not conceive. And they tried everything, even sex, but still she was barren of child. And they wept.

Then Francine went up to Mount Sinai to seek counsel from the Lord. And she went up also to a specialist at Cedars Sinai for a second opinion. And she promised the Lord that, if he would give her a child, she would give the child up in service unto the Temple for all the days of his life, though not all the evenings. And the Lord heard her prayers and answered them.

So it came to pass that she bore a son. And they called him "Murray," meaning "he whose parents have planned his life without consulting him." And they were sad no more.

chapter 11

The Early Years

———◆◆———

And when the child was weaned, his mother brought him to the Temple with three bullocks, one ephah of flour, and a box of Pampers. For though he was weaned, he was not yet toilet trained. And she said unto the High Priest of the Hebrews, "Here is the child I promised the Lord. He shall abide with thee and serve the Lord for all the days of his life, though not all the evenings."

And the High Priest of the Hebrews said, "Um, thanks but no thanks. Really. We're fine here."

And Murray went back home and remained there.

And when Murray was older, his mother

returned him to the Temple once more that he might abide there and serve the Lord. And the child did remain to minister unto the Lord before the High Priest of the Hebrews to the best of his ability, which was not great. For on parents' day, the High Priest did upbraid his mother with harsh words, saying, "Thy son speaketh barely a word of Hebrew."

And she said unto him, "Is that such a big deal?"

And the High Priest of the Hebrews answered, "At this point in history, it's our only language."

And Murray's mother was ashamed and she did weep and wail and rend her garments. And she insisted unto the High Priest that Murray was very gifted and that he just tested poorly.

Yet despite his mother's prayers for him, Murray continued to worship below his grade level until it was quietly suggested that he pursue a less demanding vocation, such as goat herding or advertising. For though he was promised to the Lord, he was a washout.

So Murray departed from the House of the Lord and went forth into the house of his parents, specifically the finished basement, where he dwelt rent-free.

And he found work among the crops in the fields, planting in the planting season and harvesting in the harvest season.

For to every thing there is a season: a time to sow, a time to reap, and a time in between to work as a bartender.

And Murray also did odd jobs in the orchards and vineyards. And though his pay was meager, Murray was content, because he was a humble person and because it was all off the books.

chapter 111

The Call of the Lord

And it came to pass that one day, while Murray was tending a small bush, lo, a sheep appeared before him. And the sheep was ablaze and aflame and also on fire. And though it burned brightly, the sheep was not consumed nor was there even the slightest aroma of lamb kebabs. And the sheep called to him and said, "Murray, Murray."

And Murray saw the sheep and asked, "What sheep art thou that thou dost burn and yet be not turned into lamb kebabs?"

And the flame-retardant sheep spake thus: "I am Yahweh, the God of your fathers, the God of Abraham, the God of Isaac, and the God of Jacob."

And Murray asked, "What dost thou wish of me?"

And he was afraid, for he sensed that this was going to involve a big favor.

And the noncombustible sheep that was the Lord said, "Son of Irving, I have chosen thee as a messenger to send to the children of Israel. For they art a rebellious nation that hath rebelled against me most rebelliously. They worship false idols and ignore my commandments. They disregard my teachings of righteousness. They omit their prayers and they neglect the temple rites. Furthermore, lately, all of their burnt offerings have been undercooked. Murray, thou shalt go unto them and cleanse my temple of its iniquity."

And Murray said, "Honestly, I thought the temple looked pretty good the last time I saw it."

And the Lord replied, "Thank you. I have someone who comes in to cleanse twice a week.

And yet, there is much iniquity if you look closely."

And Murray said, "But why me, a mere field hand and Hebrew school dropout? Shouldn't thou goest with someone with more name recognition?"

And the fire-resistant sheep answered him thus: "It is true that I, the Almighty, could transmit my message to all humanity in ways that would be direct and unmistakable. Yet I prefer to pay unexpected visits to maladjusted loners. Besides, thy mother says that you are very gifted and that you just test poorly."

And Murray said, "But what shall I say to the people? For I am not good with large crowds. I'm much better at small cocktail parties."

And the Lord answered, "Fear not, Murray, for I, the God of Israel, will be with thee. I will teach thee what to say. I will give thee strength, and the words in thy mouth shall be like fire."

"Sounds spicy," said Murray, for he had a

sensitive palate. "Surely, thou wilt also show signs and wonders and give me miracles to perform that the people might believe me?"

And the Lord said, "Now, go forth from thy land, thy birthplace, and thy parents' basement. Get thee to thy cousin Lenny, who dwelleth among the Meshuganites. He shall be thy scribe and thy amanuensis and also he shall write things down. For though he hath a masters degree, it is in comparative literature. Thus he doth labor at a plow behind twelve yoke of oxen and the smell is exceeding strong. He is open to a career move."

"Hold on," said Murray. "What about the signs and wonders?"

But the flames went out and the Lord spake no more. And the sheep, which did wander off, was not even singed.

chapter 10

INTO MESHUGANAH

———◆◆———

And it came to pass that Murray went forth to the land of the Meshuganites and found his cousin Lenny, son of Abihu, son of Elihu, son of Zehu, son of Tofu. And Lenny, though he had a masters degree in comparative literature, did indeed labor behind a team of twelve oxen.

And Murray told Lenny all that the Lord had said unto him. And Lenny thought about it and said unto Murray, "I will follow you because it is better to walk behind one ox than twelve. And because the smell here is exceeding strong."

So Murray and Lenny went out among the Meshuganites at the town gate, for it was a gated community and very exclusive. And Murray remembered the promise the Lord had made to him, that the Lord would be with him and that his words would be like fire. Wherefore he stood before the people and spake, "Hear ye the word of the Lord." And he waited for the Lord to fill him with his spirit.

But all he felt was a light breeze.

And, after a while, the crowd grew restless and the people murmured. And Murray's knees did smite each other, and his loins loosened, and his tongue cleaved to the roof of his mouth.

And when no words came to him from the Lord, he spake the only thing that came into his head, which was:

> Let there be light. Go forth and multiply.
> Buy low, sell high. Floss regularly.

And the townspeople were glad for these teachings and clamored for more.

So Murray said unto them:

The **Book** of Murray

Turn away from evil.

Be charitable unto the poor.

Love the stranger, though not on the first
date.

Always get more than one estimate.

Then he took questions and signed auto-graphs.

And from that day on, he preached again and again to all who came to hear him.

"Take not more than three suitcases for a weekend trip," he instructed them.

Share bad news quickly.

Beware of room-temperature tuna fish.

Use not a shelf without first lining it with
shelf-paper.

Rebuild not thine own carburetor.

And though Murray still awaited the word of God, yet his confidence grew. And he sang

27

praises unto God to all who would listen, saying
to the people:

> *Hear O Israel, the Lord thy God, the Lord is*
> *One.*
> *"One what?" you may ask.*
> *One heck of a God, that's what.*
> *Who is like unto Him,*
> *glorious in holiness, fearful in praises, doing*
> *wonders?*
> *Certainly no one I've ever met,*
> *though admittedly I don't get out much.*
> *How great is the Lord's dwelling place!*
> *How vast His domain, how boundless His*
> *creations,*
> *how immense the square footage!*
> *He created the beasts of the field,*
> *the birds of the air, the fishes of the sea,*
> *and every living thing that moveth upon the*
> *earth.*

In wisdom, He made them all,
except for the labradoodle, which came later.
Holy, holy, holy is the Lord of hosts.

And the people wept and prayed and kissed the hem of his garment and bathed his feet. And they anointed him with oil from the finest olive trees and garlanded him with fragrant herbs. And he smelled like salad dressing.

And with parchment, pen, and his writer's inkhorn, Lenny wrote down all the words of Murray. And he published and proclaimed them in all the cities and the streets and issued a multitude of press releases, so that surrounding Murray there was an abundance of hype.

And the people took heed and opened a chain of coffee bars where they served steamed milk, as Lenny had written, "Go froth and multiply." For though Lenny was very smart

and highly educated, he was also slightly dys-
lexic.

But the coffee bars were blessed and did
multiply and thrive. And the people were filled
with caffeine and loved Murray even more.

chapter v

The Healing of the
Hypochondriac

And a multitude came to Murray, bearing nasal inhalers and neck braces and Kleenex, beseeching him to heal them of their infirmities. And he spake unto them, saying:

> Beware the dermatologist who advertises on
>   billboards.
> Never purchase a kidney on eBay.
> Trust not a cardiologist who chain-smokes.
> Without a biopsy, it's not a real checkup.

Then he took their medical histories and made a multitude of referrals.

Now there was in the town a certain man whose head ached and who was groaning with his affliction saying, "I must have a brain tumor."

And Murray went to him and placed his hands upon him crying, "O Lord, I pray thee, heal this man."

And the man's pain went away, as if it had been only a tension headache.

And this same man had a pain in his chest and was groaning with his affliction saying, "I must be having a coronary."

And Murray went to him and placed his hands upon him crying, "O Lord, I pray thee, heal this man again, for he is truly unlucky."

And the man's chest pain went away, as if only heartburn.

And Murray healed this man of many other complaints, including but not limited to African sleeping sickness, beriberi, carpal tunnel syndrome, dropsy, the Ebola virus, flatulence, gout, hiccups, lumbago, mad cow disease, restless legs syndrome, scurvy, tennis elbow, mange, and the ague. And Murray also brought him back from the dead from time to time.

Now when they heard of these things that had been done, all the afflicted and the diseased and the lepers of the town came to Murray that he might lay hands on them and heal them too. And Murray fled from them, lest he catch something serious.

chapter vi

The Virgin by the Well

So Murray and Lenny left Meshuganah and journeyed three days until there were no cities or villages.

And they were thirsty and came to a well, but its mouth was covered with a stone and they could not move it.

And a young woman came to the well with a herd of goats for to water them. With one hand, she rolled the stone from the mouth of the well and drew water from it. Then, holding her bucket with one hand, she put the stone back with the other.

And Murray spake unto her, saying, "Maiden, what is thy name? And how much canst thou bench press?"

And the maiden was a daughter of Zion, a descendant of Mahlah, Noah, Hoglah, Milcah, and Tirzah. And she lifted her eyes unto Murray and said, "I am called Loofah."

And no man had known her. Nor had any man uncovered her nakedness, nor even gotten past first base. Except for that one time when she let a wandering Aramean get her really drunk. Still, she was not exactly well known. Nor did she date much. For she generally preferred the company of her goats.

And Loofah recognized Murray from her visits to the marketplace and from the fliers that Lenny had stapled to palm trees everywhere. And she knelt before Murray and bowed her head. And she kissed his feet and washed them with water from her bucket and dried them with her hair. And she wept. For he had journeyed far and his feet were overpowering.

Then she gave Murray and Lenny water to drink.

"Tastes like feet," said Lenny.

And Loofah watered her goats. And Murray gazed upon her and sang a song of praise:

> *Blessed be Loofah above all other women.*
> *She is comely but strong.*
> *With one hand she did move the rock from the*
>   *mouth of the well,*
> *and with one hand put it back.*
> *For her biceps are like gourds,*
> *her calves like the cedars of Lebanon,*
> *and her arms like bars of iron.*
> *Her hips are as broad as the plains of*
>   *Jericho.*
> *Yea, her bosom gives shelter like a mighty*
>   *fortress.*
> *Her skin is like unto pomegranates, reddish*
>   *and pocked, sure, but it's a delicious fruit*
>   *if you can deal with the seeds.*
> *Her raven hair is thick-perfumed with the*
>   *sweet scent of—*

"Feet," Lenny said. And he spake unto Murray, "Come, let us be on our way."

But Murray did not go, saying, "Wait! Why hasten? For I am just getting started."

And Murray said unto Loofah, "Thou art pleasing to me. May I continue?" So he sang:

> *My beloved is like a dairy goat,*
> *with velvety hide and muscular back,*
> *sturdy hocks and well-formed udders,*
> *and no sign of ringworm.*

And Loofah was well pleased by the comparison and said, "That was very beautiful, thank you."

And Murray drew near to her, and their lips met, and they kissed. And he wept. For her lips tasted like feet.

Then she said, "My lord, let me not be a stumbling block between thee and thy calling. For thou art a great prophet. And I am but a simple herdswoman. We must each stay with our own flocks. Also, we are of different tribes. For thou art a Levite and I am a Sagittarius. It could never work."

And Murray knew that she was right, and that he must go. And she knew that he knew. And he knew she knew he knew. And she knew he knew she knew he knew. So Murray knew her not, except as a friend.

And he returned to Lenny, who was waiting by the road. And Lenny said, "Murray, it is well that thou didst not know her, nor uncover her nakedness, nor even get past first base. For thou must not take a wife nor have sons or daughters.

"Being a prophet is a huge time commitment. Thou must have room in thy schedule for thy many obligations: hearing voices, going into divine trances, dreaming apocalyptic dreams, and addressing Hadassah luncheons. Speaking of which, you're booked for one next week."

And the two departed hence and went thither from that place and then they left.

chapter VII

BELSHAZZAR'S BAR MITZVAH

So Murray and Lenny went to Bethel and Goshen and Sharon. And it came to pass that when they reached Westport they came upon a great feast at the country club with one thousand guests. And Murray said, "What is this great feast?"

And the people answered, "It is Belshazzar's bar mitzvah."

And a great tent had been erected for the feast, supported by pillars topped with palm leaves and lilies and cherubim in gold. For Belshazzar's parents, the Shapiros, had more money than Yahweh.

And there was much talk of the length and breadth of the tent, it being five score cubits from end to end, which was even more cubits than the tent at the Farbman bar mitzvah.

And within the tent there were carving stations and platters heaped with the flesh of the birds of the sky and the beasts of the field, roasted au jus. There were also many fishes of the sea, smoked and served on pumpernickel.

Of the finger foods, there were four: fried, cheesy, baked-in-puff-pastry, and grilled-on-a-stick. And of accompanying dipping sauces there were a multitude. And that was just the hors d'oeuvres.

Thus the invited guests did marvel at the feast, and some said it was very ritzy while others said it was fancy-shmancy. And all did eat and celebrate until they were satisfied, though later they complained about everything.

And Belshazzar received many tributes and the people gloried in his name, which was also printed on all the cocktail napkins. They gave him presents, gift certificates, and personal checks, and he accepted all major credit cards.

chapter viii

The Writing on the Wall

But in the same hour, the Lord sent a stormy wind and rain and there appeared a mysterious writing on the wall. And who drew it they knew not, but they were pretty sure it was not part of the bar mitzvah's theme, which was skateboarding.

And the Shapiros summoned from among all the invited guests the wisest ones: the conjurors, the soothsayers, the astrologers, and the management consultants. And they asked them, "Canst thou interpret this writing on the wall?"

But none could.

Then said the party planner, "There is in the kingdom a man, a great prophet, who is filled with the holy spirit. He hath great understanding and wisdom and can explain the meaning of this thing."

"What is his name? Bring him to me," said Mr. Shapiro.

And the party planner said, "His name is Daniel. Unfortunately, he is booked for the Cohens' Sweet Sixteen. But I'm hearing good things about a prophet named Murray, whom I see over by the chocolate fountain."

And they went unto the chocolate fountain and asked Murray, "Dost thou know the meaning of the writing on the wall?"

Now when Murray saw the writing, he recognized none of the words. And he called unto the Lord for a translation, but none came. And he was dismayed.

And as the Shapiros waited for his answer, a hush fell upon the room, and the eyes of all the assembled guests were upon him.

Soon they began to murmur, "He doesn't know what it means, does he?"

And Lenny whispered, "Thou shouldst probably say something. For thou art losing them."

And Murray said, "But what shall I say? For they art a tough crowd."

But Lenny said, "Remind them of their sins. Tell them of the sacred covenant of their fathers which they have broken. Warn them of the awful wrath of the Almighty. Describe the terrible consequences that will certainly befall them if they do not repent of their evil ways. Above all, keep it light."

And seeing he could delay no longer, Murray spake thus:

> Children of Israel, the day of thy calamity is upon thee! The righteous judgment of the Lord is at hand! His punishment will be swift and terrible!

And at that moment, the wind and rain grew stronger so that the whole tent shook and swayed.

And Lenny gave him a thumbs-up, and whispered, "Thou art doing great!"

And Murray continued:

> The Lord delights not in thy feast, nor in the melody of thy lyres, nor in the ca-lypso songs of thy Caribbean steel drum band.
>
> Thy party motivators, celebrity imper-sonators, sweatshirt makers, and glass-blowers are a trouble unto him.
>
> Thy raw bar he abhors.
>
> If he hath to see one more video mon-tage, he will send another flood, for he is weary to bear them.
>
> Yea, he hath had it up to here, and the day of reckoning is nigh!

Verily, He will smite thee seven times for thy pride, seven times more for thy iniquity, and seven times again for thy fashion sense. Which I believe comes to twenty-one times, though I am a prophet, not a math person.

Thy fasting will not impress Him, neither will thy feasting, nor thy fasting then feasting then fasting, nor any other eating disorder.

Shame will be upon thy faces and Botox will not make it go away. He will take away thy bracelets and anklets and earrings. The nose jobs you can keep.

Howl ye, but He will answer not thy prayers.

But before I go on, I'd like to take a moment to congratulate our bar mitzvah boy Belshazzar. For though I have never met this fine young man, I feel like I've known him my whole life. What a great job you've done here today, Belshazzar! Though perhaps all the standing ovations you received were a bit excessive.

And how about a shout-out to the Shapiros, who spared no effort or expense to throw this shindig? Sadly, what with thy trespasses and transgressions and broken covenant and all, it will probably be thy last.

And there was much murmuring, and the assembled guests whispered, "Who invited him?"

Then Murray said, "Now, this is the writing that was written:

MENE MENE TEKEL
UPHARSIN

And this is the interpretation of the thing:

MENE—Thy days are numbered. The end is near. Repent now! For sackcloth will be the new black.

TEKEL—The Lord hath weighed you in the balances and you have been found wanting. The Lord suggests you try cutting out sugar and maybe eat less dairy.

UPHARSIN—If this is a thirteenth birthday party, what do you do for weddings?

And some whispered, "Does it really say that?" for they were skeptical.

And others answered, "No, I don't believe it says that."

And still others muttered, "I've had better prophecies from fortune cookies."

But Mrs. Shapiro said, "He makes a good point. For our daughter Tiffany's wedding, we're going to have to start thinking big."

And Mr. Shapiro was surprised by his wife's words but said nothing, for upon hearing them he began choking on his food.

And while Mr. Shapiro was receiving the Heimlich maneuver, the rains kept falling upon the earth so that the tent became soaked. And more letters emerged on the wet cloth until all could see the complete writing, which was:

MENAHEM'S TENTS TWENTY SHEKELS
AND UP THE ALL-WEATHER SOLUTION

Among all who saw it, a few said it was the work of the Lord. But most said it looked like a stencil. And their anger was kindled against Murray. And all were agreed that he would never work another bar mitzvah again.

And Lenny shook his head and said, "Verily, this is a PR nightmare."

And when Murray saw the writing, he fled and made great haste away. For he feared that there would be a stoning, in which case he would be stoned to death with stones.

chapter 15

THE PASSION OF MURRAY

So it came to pass that Murray went up into the wilderness because he was in despair, and because he had no sense of direction.

He brought with him no victual or provision, and also he had no food. For he had fled in such haste that he had neglected to take with him even a rugelach from the Viennese table.

And he was like a voice that crieth in the wilderness, for he was, technically, in the wilderness and he was crying most of the time.

And he came unto the mountains and lodged in a cave, praying to the Lord for forty days and forty nights.

There, he was fed by ravens, which brought

him bread and flesh in the morning and bread and flesh in the evening, until finally he said, "What, bread and flesh again?"

But there was no other delivery service in the area.

And on the fortieth day, he heard a voice calling to him, saying "Murray, Murray."

And Murray went outside from the cave and onto a ledge and cried: "Lord, is that You?"

But there was only silence. So he went on:

> From the depths I have called to Thee, yet Thou taketh not my calls. Wherefore hast Thou brought me hither? Whither am I to go now?
>
> Lo these many years I have been Thy humble servant, obeying Thy summons to be Thy prophet. Yet when I seek Thy help, or any hint or sign, thou art absent,

AWOL, gone fishing. Why hidest Thou
Thy face from me?

Behold, after all this time, still I wot not
a whit of what Thou listeth. Frankly, I
don't even know what I just said. Why
dost Thou have us talk like this? Are we
Amish?

And a great wind rent the mountain, but
the Lord was not in the wind. And after the
wind, there was an earthquake, but the Lord
was not in the earthquake. And after the earthquake, there was a fire; but the Lord was not in
the fire.

And Murray, who had been waiting patiently, began to grow restless. And he paced
and whistled on the ledge, did stretching exer-
cises and calisthenics and, scanning the horizon,
noted to himself, "This is some view!"

But finally, after the fire, there was a still, small voice. And the still, small voice said unto him, "Murray, I'm sorry, but we need the cave. We have another prophet arriving at noon."

chapter x

The Descent from the Mountain

So Murray took leave of the mountain. And his spirits were low as he made the long journey down, for he knew not where to turn next.

And when he reached the bottom, he was weary and thirsty and covered with dust. And he came upon a camp tended by a goatherd dressed in a garment of goatskins. And lo, it was Loofah, who was building a campfire out of goat dung.

And he embraced her and said, "Beloved, thy smell is as a freshly fertilized field."

And she thanked him and said, "It's good to see you too."

And when the fire was built, she cooked a mess of pottage.

And he told her all that had come to pass and said, "Woe is me. I am finished. For the people's anger is kindled against me. They will never incline their ears to my words but will scorn me with scorn and rebuke me with re-bukes. And why shouldn't they? For the Lord hath forgotten me. Therefore let me remain here with you and the goats."

And Loofah said, "Make not a big decision on an empty stomach. Here, let us eat of the mess I have made."

So they ate of the mess, and tears streamed down Murray's face. And he asked, "What is this mess?"

For it was a pottage of garlic, onions, peppers, and horseradish. And his nasal passages had never been so clear.

And when they were finished, Loofah said to him gently, "Murray, O holy man, it would content me greatly for you to stay. For other than my goats, there is no one I would rather converse with.

"But thou must return to thy people to spread the word of the Living God. For the Lord called thee to be His holy messenger to the children of Israel. And if thou disobeyest Him, He will rip thee a new one.

"When thou speakest to the multitudes, perhaps they will not hearken diligently to thy words. But later, when thy prophecy is fulfilled, thou canst say to them, 'See? I told thee so! But didst thou hearken diligently? No! And whose fault was that?'

"And the people will say, 'Yea, verily, he is annoying. But he is right.'

"And it will give thee much satisfaction.

"Take heart and be of good courage. For thy work is like this dung fire I have built. It burns low, yet the embers have not gone out. Behold!"

And Loofah added a handful of turds to the

glowing embers, and flames rose up and consumed them. And the fire crackled and roared.

"Thine own fire has not yet gone out either," she said unto him. "Arise, go forth, and add more turds to it!"

And Murray was stirred by her words. And he said, "I will do it. I will add more turds. But where shall I find them?"

And Loofah answered, "Fear not, for they are everywhere. The Lord will provide."

And Murray said, "Praised be the Lord for sending thee to me. Blessed be thy advice, which has kept me from abandoning my calling this day. For who can find one such as thee?"

And Murray sang to her a song of praise:

> *Praised be Loofah, woman of valor!*
> *Strength and dignity are her clothing.*
> *Also animal skins.*
> *She herdeth her goats and, with her bare*
>   *hands,*

The 𝕭𝖔𝖔𝖐 of Murray

buildeth a fire of dung.

She cooketh a savory pottage to unblock any

  sinus,

washing her hands first, one hopeth.

She speaketh encouraging words,

using helpful visual aids.

Her own works praise her,

saying "Blee-eh" and "Meh!"

for they are goats, with a limited vocabulary.

Yea, who can find such a woman?

Her price is far above rubies,

figuratively speaking, of course.

And she was deeply moved.

chapter #1

THE TEN (OR SO) COMMANDMENTS

———◆◆◆———

And the next morning Murray went out from the camp and came upon Lenny. And a multitude of the children of Israel was gathered in the plain.

And Lenny said unto him, "Verily, thou hast had a bad break. But despair not. For I have found for thee a new booking. It could be thy big comeback."

And Murray said unto Lenny, "Wherefore is this multitude of the children of Israel gathered in the plain?"

And Lenny said, "Their temple dismissed their rabbi three years ago and the search committee still cannot agree upon a replacement. Go and preach unto them."

And Murray said, "You remembereth last time."

But Lenny said, "Fear not, for they are dissatisfied with everyone. It is the ideal opportunity for thee. Just be prophetic and try not to say anything that can actually be checked."

Then thick clouds descended upon the mountain and there were thunders and lightnings. And the mountain smoked.

And the multitude shook and trembled and some among them said, "Verily, this is not good beach weather."

And others among them said, "I thought this was a nonsmoking mountain."

Then there was the sound of trumpet blasts exceeding loud. And Murray called the people to hearken unto him. And they gathered solemnly at his feet, each man and woman standing before him alone, accompanied only by their families, au pairs, personal trainers, life coaches, tutors, psychiatrists, financial advisers, nutritionists, physical therapists, allergists, personal shoppers, feng shui consultants, and Kabbalah instructors.

And Murray spake unto them saying, "Sinful sinners, you have sinned a great sin. You have forgotten the simple commandments that the Lord gave to Moses on Mount Sinai and that Moses gave to thine ancestors."

Then Murray paused, for he could not remember them either.

Then he resumed:

> Now these were the commandments that were commanded:
>
> I am the Lord thy God, which brought thee out of the land of Egypt, where I sent thee to be enslaved in the first place. Be grateful and don't ask questions.
>
> Thou shalt have no strange gods before me. I am thy one and only strange god.

Thou shalt make no graven or molten images. And no flash photography! For the Lord thy God is a camera-shy god.

Thou shalt not take the name of the Lord Thy God in vain without the express written consent of the Lord Thy God. The Lord Thy God® is a registered trademark of The Lord Thy God. Any use of the name of the Lord Thy God without the express written consent of the Lord Thy God is an abomination that the Lord Thy God will punish unto the generations. For permissions and licensing, contact The Lord Thy God.

Remember the Sabbath day to keep it holy. It's every weekend.

On this day thou shalt do no work. For in six days the Lord created the heavens and the earth. And He saw what He had made and, behold, it was good. On the Seventh Day, He rested. And on the Eighth Day, He took another look and asked, "But is it good for the Jews?"

Honor thy father and thy mother but screen thy calls.

Thou shalt not kill without an alibi. Thou shalt not go postal.

Then Murray concluded, "Those were the commandments that the Lord handed down to Moses after the exodus from Egypt. He wrote them on two tablets of stone and added no more."

And Lenny whispered unto Murray, "That was only six. Seven, at most. I believe there were ten."

And Murray spake unto the multitude, saying, "But wait. I almost forgot:

Thou hast the right to an attorney. If thou canst not afford an attorney, one will be appointed for thee."

And Lenny shook his head, saying, "That wasn't one of them."

And Murray added:

> Thou shalt not return clothes to a store after wearing them to a job interview.

> Thou shalt not Google thy symptoms and then phone thy internist at two A.M. claiming to have a terminal illness.

> Thou shalt not intentionally omit ingredients when sharing recipes.

And Lenny shook his head again.

And Murray reflected for a moment, and continued:

> Thou shalt not commit adultery on JDate.

> Thou shalt not steal. Thou shalt not embezzle if thou art a Hassidic rabbi, for that looks especially bad.

The 𝕭𝖔𝖔𝖐 of Murray

Thou shalt not bear false witness against thy neighbor. Neither shalt thou be an expert witness against thy neighbor. In general, try to stay out of litigation against thy neighbor.

Thou shalt not covet thy neighbor's wife, nor his house, flocks, fields, or servants. For thou shalt love thy neighbor. But thou shalt not tell thy neighbor of thy love, lest he get the wrong idea.

And Murray whispered to Lenny, "How many was that?"

And Lenny answered, "Fifteen? Sixteen? I'm not sure. You can stop anytime."

chapter #11

THE FURTHER NOODGING
OF MURRAY

But Murray continued. And these were the additional statutes, judgments, and unwanted advice of Murray:

Thou shalt not put anything in writing.

Thou shalt get everything in writing.

Thou shalt not treat the Jewish high holidays as an opportunity to stay home and wait for the cable guy.

Thou shalt not mountain-climb, spelunk, or skydive.

Thou shalt not be a roofer, stunt driver, or rodeo clown.

Thou shalt not freelance.

Neither shalt thou be an optometrist. For they are not real doctors.

Thou shalt not be intimate with a woman and her daughter. Or a woman and her son's daughter. Or thy wife and thy wife's sister. How canst thou even keep track of all this?

When a great sage dies, thou shalt not ask, "Who got his apartment?"

Thou shalt not trim the corners of thy beard. Neither shalt thou comb the corners of thy beard over thy head to cover thy bald spot.

Thou shalt not mess up the guest towels in the guest bathroom. Yea, not even if thou art the guest.

Thou shalt tithe not less than one tenth
of thine income to the Lord. Fifteen to
twenty percent if the service has been
particularly good.

Thou shalt harbor no grudge against
thy neighbor. Thou shalt get even with
thy neighbor quickly.

Thou shalt not be overdressed.

That shalt not be underdressed.

Thou shalt not not worry.

Thou shalt always make things sound
worse than they are.

Thou shalt not mumble.

So Murray commanded these commandments, and Lenny copied all of them down.
And among the assembled multitude, many

said they would remember and do them and make them an eternal covenant, for their hearts were humbled.

But some felt the adoption of the commandments should be put to a vote of the entire congregation.

And others wanted to appoint a committee to study the pros and cons of each commandment and issue a detailed report.

So a motion was made to vote on whether to put the commandments to a vote. And the motion was debated, with a multitude of points of order. Then a motion was made to table the motion to vote on whether to put the commandments to a vote. And that motion carried.

Then, by unanimous consent, they adjourned for lunch.

chapter 𝔵111

THE MURRAY DIET

———◆—◆◆—◆———

And when Murray and Lenny saw that the children of Israel were having lunch, they had lunch as well. For Loofah had followed and brought them victuals.

So they drank sour goat's milk from goat skins. And they ate goat yogurt, goat cheese, goat curds, curdled goat curds, and goat curd fondue.

And Lenny said, "Tastes like feet."

And while the children of Israel were eating their own lunches, Murray took the opportunity to speak unto them, saying:

These are the commandments that the Lord thy God hath commanded with respect to food:

It shall be a perpetual statute unto thy people that ye shall not make thyself abominable with any abominable thing.

Ye shall eat of the good carbs and shall eat not of the bad carbs. Ye shall eat not of the fat, especially not of the trans fat.

Ye shall eat of the proteins and the green leafy vegetables rich in antioxidants. Ye shall eat also of the fruits and of the whole grains. But not of the Froot Loops. For they are Froot Loops. And ye shall not eat of them.

And these are the beasts of the field which ye may eat: the cow, the sheep, the goat, and the brisket.

These are the beasts ye may not eat: the squirrel, the possum, the varmint, and the critter. Neither shall ye eat of any beast with tire marks on it.

Of the fish, ye may eat of the salmon, the carp, the herring, and the gefilte.

Ye may eat of the trout but ye shall not fly-fish for it. Ye did not cross the Red Sea on dry land so that ye could wade into a river up to thy belly button.

Of the birds, ye may eat of the chicken, every single night.

Ye may eat also of the turkey, which shall be overcooked.

Ye may eat of the duck, the grouse, and the quail, but ye shall not go hunting for them, lest ye accidentally put thine eye out. For thee, *duck, grouse,* and *quail* shall mainly be verbs.

David M. Bader

The creatures of which ye may eat shall be organic; free range; wild; grass-fed; non–genetically modified; mercury-, hormone-, and antibiotic-free; and represented by counsel.

Of the tofu, ye may eat, if ye desireth. It is thine own call.

Ye shall eat no manner of McNugget. For it is a McNugget. Therefore ye shall not eat of it.

Of the bagel, ye may eat of the plain, sesame, poppy seed, salt, cinnamon-raisin, garlic, and pumpernickel, yea even unto the "everything" bagel. But ye shall not eat of the sourdough-blueberry-pesto bagel.

Ye shall not mix meat, dairy, and artificial sweeteners. Ye shall not order a cheeseburger with fries and then ask for a Sweet'N Low.

The deep-fried Twinkie, it shall not be eaten. For it is a Twinkie. And it is deep-fried. And ye shall not eat it.

At a restaurant, ye shall not remain at the first table offered thee but shall ask to be seated elsewhere.

Though the menu sayeth "No Substitutions," yet ye shall ask for substitutions.

Ye shall not eat the food served to thee but shall say, "This is ice cold!" and send it back.

At a Chinese restaurant, ye shall not order the Szechuan Chicken with Red Chilies in Hot Bean Sauce without also asking, "Can you make it not too spicy?"

David M. Bader

Ye shall not return to a restaurant until one year has passed, lest the staff remember you.

Of the sandwiches, ye may eat of the cold cuts on rye with mustard or Russian dressing. But of the Potato-Chips-with-Miracle-Whip-on-Wonderbread sandwich, ye shall not eat. For it is an abomination. And ye shall not eat it.

Ye shall not eat half-price sushi. For it is sushi at half-price. And ye shall not eat it.

Ye shall eat family-style with thy family. And there shall be yelling. For it is family-style.

Ye shall not eat every dish and side dish, though it be included in the Early Bird Special.

And if ye overindulgeth or snacketh between meals, woe unto you. For though it spendeth a moment on thy lips yea, verily, it spendeth an eternity on thy hips.

And these were the commandments which Murray commanded with respect to food. And they were known as The Murray Diet.

And the children of Israel said they would obey them and make them an everlasting regimen, starting next week.

For they had already tried the Forbidden Fruit Diet, the Seven Years of Famine Diet, the Seven-Day Bread of Affliction Diet, the Manna and Quail Diet, the Day of Atonement Crash Diet, and the All-Kugel Diet. And still the children of Israel could not get rid of their love-handles.

chapter xiv

The Vision of Murray

𝕬nd after lunch, the thunder and lightning resumed and the trumpets sounded. And the people muttered, "Again with the trumpets."

But they gathered around and listened. And these were the words that Murray spake unto them:

> Hear ye, O Children of Israel, the Lord chose thee to be a peculiar people unto himself. But not too peculiar. Ye need not overdo it.

> For the Lord thy God is a kind and loving God. But He is also a jealous God and avenging. Slow to anger but of great

might. Passive-aggressive yet controlling. In a word, difficult. And He will love thee unconditionally, subject to certain conditions.*

And the righteous among you who follow his commandments will be entered into the Book of Life. But the wicked will be entered into the Book of Death. For like any good businessman, God keeps more than one set of books.

And He will inscribe who will live and who will die, who by fire, who by water,

---

*One entry per person. Offer void in the following states: Persia, Assyria, Babylonia, Louisiana. Offer may not be combined with offers from other deities. No purchase necessary, fasting and prayers always appreciated. Prizes not transferable. Awards may be delayed in the event of calamities, natural disasters, and other Acts of God. God is not liable for damages caused by Acts of God. Other restrictions may apply. For complete rules, consult the unknowable mind of God.

who by sword, who by famine, and who by massive coronary on the tennis court.

Yea, if thou hearken not to Him, curses will overtake thee. He will set his face against thee and chastise thee and punish thee. And he will not acquit the guilty, except on occasion when they are represented by Alan Dershowitz.

He will smite thee with plagues and famine and pestilence until thy houses are without inhabitant.

And some will say, "How doth the city sit solitary that was full of people!"

And others will say, "I think they moved to the suburbs."

The point is, He will make thy land a desolation, which will hurt property values.

He will tread upon thy high places and upon thy low places and upon the carpeting. Thou wilt cry unto the Lord and lament with great lamentation but it will avail thee not.

For He will answer, "Stop thy lamenting or I'll really give thee something to lament about."

And He will insist that it hurts Him more than it hurts thee.

And He will burden ye with heavy burdens, and ye shall slouch and sag beneath their weight. And thy shoulders will stay that way, proving thy mother correct, which will be even worse than thy heavy burdens.

Yea, verily, ye shall be dispersed in a two-thousand-year exile. Everywhere thou goest, thou wilt find slander, oppression, destruction, persecution, and exile.

Also cruelty, calamity, misery, and tribulations.

And hardship, injustice, and despair.

Therefore, dress warmly and wear layers. Empty thy bladder before fleeing. Bring sunblock, an extra pair of eyeglasses, and hard candies. Learn useful foreign phrases like, "I see you have set our village on fire," and "We'll be running for our lives now." Avoid unwashed fruit.

And though thou wilt be enslaved, persecuted, and downtrodden for centuries, look on the bright side. For though the Lord will destroy you, later he will redeem you and bless you.

For that is just the kind of deity He is, visiting destruction one day, pardoning and forgiving iniquity the next. Truly He is gracious and good, all-loving, all-powerful, and all-merciful, just with these mood swings.

And He will raise up His ruins and rebuild them as in the days of old. On that day, every valley shall be exalted, every mountain and hill shall be made low, the crooked shall be made straight and the rough places plain.

And the long-suffering people who were brought down low will be raised up high. And those who were proud and lofty will be brought down low. And then those who were brought down low will once more be raised up high. And then low again, and then high. But then low.

And the deaf shall hear, the blind shall
see, the meek shall increase their joy,
and the poor among men shall rejoice.
Oh to be deaf, blind, meek, and poor!

He will make the desert bloom and
make the dry land a spring of water.
And it will be called Las Vegas. And
there will be low air fares and package
deals and entertainment nightly.

And among the congregation many whispered, "Las Vegas?"

But Murray continued:

And from the stock of Jesse will come a
savior. And the stock of Jesse (NASDAQ:
JESS) will rise ten points on the rumors.

And He will assemble the outcasts of Israel, and gather together the dispersed
of the four corners of the earth into

one place, where they shall barely be on speaking terms. And that place shall be called Brooklyn.

And thou shalt set up houses of worship in every city and suburb. And they shall be like unto the Temple of Solomon, if Solomon had been fond of poured-concrete polyhedrons.

And on that day, all the frozen food in thy refrigerator—the pot roasts, the soups, the casseroles, the matzoh balls, the kreplach, the babkas, and the macaroons—shall be thawed. And they shall be like unto lead weights and just as digestible. But they shall not be fatal. For the Lord thy God is a merciful God.

And thy tenements and sweatshops shall become lofts and boutiques. And pickles and knishes shall be scarce, but there shall be martinis in abundance and dogs that fit in handbags.

And ye shall return also to the land of thy fathers and put prayer-filled notes in the cracks of the "wailing wall" of thine ancient temple. And the Lord shall read some of them with dismay. For the Almighty, blessed be He, dislikes "From the desk of . . ." stationery.

And thy people will produce philoso-phers and scientists and novelists and filmmakers and composers and chess masters and Nobel prize winners. Yet still thou wilt be unable to find the hood release on thy car.

And as Murray prophesied and wailed and wrung his hands, Lenny handed out pledge cards. And when Murray had concluded, all agreed that it had been an excellent sermon.

And those who had been snoring throughout were especially vocal in their praise. And the people told their friends who told their friends. And the news of Murray's return went out into all the lands.

chapter xv

THE WISDOM OF MURRAY

And the people praised Murray and said he must be approved of God because of all the great things that he had done. For in the accounts of his recent accomplishments there had been some exaggeration.

It was claimed that he had fed an entire multitude with a single bagel.

It was also claimed that he had miraculously turned water into wine. And it was said that when the wine turned out to be Manischewitz Extra Heavy Malaga, he had quickly turned it back into water.

And it was claimed that he commanded the sun to stand still overhead a full day. Though a few insisted that it just seemed to be standing still while he was speaking.

Thus Murray added many new followers who believed in him, as well as others who did not believe but followed him anyway because their mothers had said, "Go, you might meet someone."

And the people flocked to him and beseeched him to hear their disputes and judge them.

And it came to pass that there were two women who had a dispute, and they appeared before Murray. And one said unto him, "O wise man, I and this woman dwell in one house. And we are roommates, splitting the rent fifty-fifty. Though she took the larger room with the walk-in closet and helpeth not with the chores.

"Now I had purchased a black-and-white cookie in the marketplace, intending to have it for breakfast the next day. And yea, I know, it was not nutritious, yet verily I was looking forward to it.

"But when I awoke in the morning, my black-and-white cookie was gone. And when I searched, I found it in the hands of my roommate. For she had taken it and was about to eat it herself."

Then her roommate spoke up, saying to Murray, "Nay, it is lies, all lies. The cookie is mine."

And Murray said, "This woman sayeth the black-and-white cookie is hers. But her roommate sayeth that, no, it is hers."

And he was perplexed.

So he conferred with Lenny at some length. Then he said unto the crowd that had gathered, "Bring me a kitchen knife."

And they did.

And Murray said, "Let the black-and-white cookie be divided down the middle. One shall have the portion with the vanilla icing, and the other shall have the portion with the chocolate icing."

And he raised the knife.

And the woman who had yearned for her missing cookie said unto Murray, "I pray you, divide not the cookie. Better to let her have the whole thing than to separate the two icings."

Though her roommate readily acquiesced to Murray's solution.

Then Murray said, "The first woman is the rightful owner. Give her the whole cookie. For her roommate knoweth nothing of black-and-white cookies."

And the people heard the decision and were in awe. And they knew that he had judged with just judgment and was very wise.

And Murray gave many proverbs to the people, instructing them thus:

> A soft answer turneth away wrath, but a
> good lawyer preventeth litigation.

Worshipping multiple deities doth not improve thine odds. Besides, monotheism saves time.

No man entereth the same river twice, unless he refuseth to ask for directions.

He that spareth the rod hateth his child, but he that nameth his child Lexington Dakota Schwartz hateth his child even more.

Man who is born of woman is born to trouble. Man who is not born of woman has other issues.

Move not to a town where a penitentiary is the main source of employment.

When a serial killer cometh from a Jewish family, always ask, "Wasn't he adopted?"

Brave is he who trieth the cheeseburger at an all-dairy kosher restaurant.

David M. Bader

Trust not the divinations of false prophets or the calorie claims of frozen-yogurt franchises.

A combination anticavity toothpaste and whitener will do neither job well.

One who thinks *kosher* means "clean" hath not bought a Hebrew National hot dog from a street vendor.

Where there is no vision, the people perish. Where there is some vision, the people cannot parallel park.

It is better to have a delicatessen sandwich named after thyself than a disease.

The Lord giveth wisdom unto the wise and knowledge to them that know understanding. For He never knoweth what to get people.

The 𝕭𝖔𝖔𝖐 of Murray

Seek not greatness for thyself and desire not honor. But pursue them anyway for it will give thy parents such pleasure.

Remember thy Creator in the days of thy youth, that thou may knowest whom to complain to later.

chapter xvi

THE DREAM OF KING JOE BOB

ow at that time, the land was ruled by kings who contended in battle with many nations that warred against them. Wherefore their reigns tended to be quite short.

And it came to pass that Aminadab was King, and he reigned and fought and died of his wounds. Then Abinadab reigned in his stead and he too fought and died of his wounds.

And after Aminadab and Abinadab came Jehonadab and Jonadab. Then Nodab and Nadab. Then Joab, Jobab, and Joe Bob. And each reigned and fought and died of his wounds—except the last. King Joe Bob reigned and fought, but he did not die of his wounds. In fact, he received no wounds at all and generally gave wounds to others.

For King Joe Bob was a mighty man of war who delighted in spilling blood. It was said that Saul slew his thousands and David his tens of thousands, but that King Joe Bob once slew a man just to watch him give up the ghost. And he was an ornery king.

And it came to pass that King Joe Bob dreamed a dream that did trouble his spirits, so that he woke up with a disquieting premonition of doom. Therefore he said unto his counselors, "Counselors, I have dreamed a dream that did trouble my spirits, so that I woke up with a disquieting premonition of doom."

And he said that if any of them could explain it, that person would be the honored guest at King Joe Bob's Annual Barbecue, Hoedown, and Festival of the First Fruits.

But if that person should fail, King Joe Bob

himself would personally smite, slay, and hew him to pieces.

And when none accepted his offer, King Joe Bob was wroth and ordered them to find him someone else to interpret his dream, else he would smite, slay, and hew them all to pieces anyway. And with one voice, they recommended Murray.

So the King sent a captain of fifty mighty men, along with the mighty men, unto Murray to summon him.

And Lenny greeted the captain and said, "The Prophet Murray can see thee three weeks from Thursday, though he may have a cancellation before then if thou wouldst like to be placed on the waiting list."

So it came to pass that, later that day, Murray and Lenny were brought before King Joe Bob in manacles and leg irons.

And King Joe Bob thanked Murray for

coming to see him. Then he spake, "Murray, son of Irving, it is said that thou canst understand a dream to interpret it. Yea, verily, it is said that thou canst even interpret dreams within dreams, like when thou thinkest thou hast woken up from a dream but thou art only dreaming that thou hast woken up and thou art actually still fast asleep."

For the land was rife with tales of Murray's amazing powers. But before Murray could set the record straight, King Joe Bob continued, "Therefore, if thou canst explain my dream, thou wilt be the honored guest at my Annual Barbecue, Hoedown, and Festival of the First Fruits. But if not, I will personally smite, slay, and hew thee to pieces."

And Murray thanked him and said that it was a great opportunity for which any prophet would be glad, but that he must respectfully decline.

"Contrary to what you may have heard, dreams are really not my specialty," Murray explained, adding that he and Lenny had truly enjoyed their visit and would be on their way just as soon as their manacles and leg irons were removed.

And King Joe Bob nodded and said, "Now, behold, this is the dream I have dreamed: I am attending a great banquet when suddenly a creature approaches me."

And Murray asked, "A four-headed creature with the faces of an ox, an eagle, a lion, and a man? With horns and wings and teeth of iron?"

For he hoped it might be one of those dreams. Dreams of four-headed creatures with horns and wings and teeth of iron were not uncommon, usually brought on by late-night snacks of spicy falafel.

But King Joe Bob said, "No, the creature approaching me at the banquet is a small, well-dressed woman who doth introduce herself as Mrs. Stein, a fundraiser for the United Judean Appeal.

"And she sayeth that for five hundred shekels I can be a donor at the Court of Solomon level and receive a fourteen-karat gold lapel pin.

"And I try to excuse myself when, behold, an identical woman approacheth and sayeth that, for a donation of five thousand shekels, I can upgrade to the House of David level, which includeth a horsedrawn carriage ride plus two orchestra seats for the hit musical *Deuteronomy!*

"And I try to flee but, behold, my path is blocked by yet another Mrs. Stein, who offereth that, for just fifty thousand shekels, I would be at their highest level, a Close Personal Friend of Moses. With that, I receive a trip to the Holy Land, a group tour of the major sites, and a spa day at the Dead Sea.

"And I reply, 'Are you mad? I already dwelleth in the Holy Land!' Though the spa day soundeth appealing.

"Then I ask what their minimum contribution is.

"And as one, they sayeth, 'That would be our lowest donor level, the King Joe Bob. It cometh with a tote bag. It is so low that, frankly, we'd like to do away with it completely.'

"And they nod and laugh.

"And I protest, 'But I myself am King Joe Bob, a mighty man of war! How dare thee! I should smite, slay, and hew thee to pieces!'

"But it availeth nothing, for when I speak, no words come out. And they weep with laughter, exclaiming, 'King Joe Bob!' and 'Tote bag!' and their laughter grows louder and louder. And then I wake up."

And Murray listened patiently and stroked his chin and said, "O King, I'm sorry but I'm not getting anything. Are you sure none of them had horns or wings?"

But King Joe Bob shook his head, saying, "No, definitely no horns or wings. Just the laughter. The laughter!"

And the King was much vexed.

And seeing that the King was much vexed and that the men of King Joe Bob were gripping their sword handles more tightly, Lenny was afraid that both he and Murray would surely be put to death. But he had listened attentively to the dream and whispered a few words to Murray. And Murray heard him and nodded.

And Murray asked King Joe Bob, "O King, I pray thee, what was Mrs. Stein's first name? Was it Phyllis?"

And the King thought and said, "Possibly. Yea, verily, it was! Not Mrs. Stein—Phyllis Stein."

And Murray said, "So in thy dream thou art beset by a Phyllis Stein. Who wants to do away with you. Yea, by a number of people named

Phyllis Stein who want to do away with you.
Nope . . . I'm still not getting anything."

Then it was Lenny who was much vexed,
and he whispered to Murray again with such
vehemence that Murray's ears rang. And
Murray finally got his drift.

And Murray said, "O King, thy dream, here
is the meaning of it: Thou art encircled by the
tribe of Philistines who take a dim view of you.
They are a great multitude and would like to
do away with you altogether. Now, therefore, let
King Joe Bob call up an army of men and pre-
pare his defenses."

So King Joe Bob heeded Murray's counsel,
and he called up an army of men. And King Joe
Bob went out among his men and said, "Arise!
We are to fight the tribe of Phyllis Steins, who
aim to destroy us. And beware, for though they
appear to be small, well-dressed Jewish women,
yet they are feisty and tenacious."

For King Joe Bob did not entirely grasp the situation.

And it came to pass that when the host of the actual Philistines arrayed themselves in battle, King Joe Bob was surprised at their appearance. But God delivered them into his hands anyway, and he and his men slaughtered thousands of hundreds.

And King Joe Bob personally struck many men with the edge of his sword and thrust them through and smote, slew, and hewed them to pieces, so that the earth was soaked with their blood.

And afterward, he was finally able to sleep soundly.

So it came to pass that, as the King had promised, Murray was an honored guest at the Annual Barbecue, Hoedown, and Festival of First Fruits.

For it was commanded that, every year, the people take the unblemished firstlings of their herds that were male and sacrifice them unto the Lord. Wherefore all the invitations said "BYOB" (Bring Your Own Bull). And the people brought their own bulls and barbecued them unto the Lord.

As was also commanded, the people took the first fruits of the harvest and gave these to the high priest of the Temple as an offering. But any that were soft or dented they kept and mixed in blender drinks and baked into pies unto the Lord.

And there was a great feast at which, as the guest of honor, Murray was obligated to sample all the food and drink. Then the people danced riotously and lifted Murray's chair off the ground and kept him aloft as they reveled.

And when they finally put him down, Murray said unto Lenny, "I have been young and now I am old, and yet never have I felt so queasy."

And King Joe Bob praised Murray and robed

him in scarlet, and Murray thanked him. And at an opportune moment Murray and Lenny departed from that place in peace as quickly as they could.

And when they were some distance away, they ran and did not look back. And they vowed a solemn vow that, in the future, they would try to keep a lower profile.

chapter XVII

The Peak Earning Years
of Murray

———◆·◆·◆———

And it came to pass that, after many years, Murray grew weary of preaching and prophesying. And he said unto Lenny, "Vanity of vanities, all is vanity. What profit have we in all our labor taken under the sun? The sun ariseth and the sun goeth down. One generation passeth away, another cometh. Bellbottoms are in, then they're out, then they're in again. Same with thin neckties and lava lamps. Behold, it is all empty, meaningless, a vexation of spirit."

And Lenny took these words to heart. Then he crunched some numbers and said unto Murray, "Profit-wise, we've actually done quite well from all our labor."

For Lenny had known this day would come

and had planned ahead. While Murray was instructing followers on the importance of having a good name, Lenny had made lucrative use of Murray's.

There was Murray's Balm-in-Gilead Skin Replenishing Gel. ("Used by the anointed one of God! It doesn't just anointeth—it sootheth and moisturizeth deep down.")

And Murray's Orthopedic Sandals. ("Not just for wandering prophets! Now everyone can walk in the way of the Lord—in comfort.")

And Murray's Extra-Strength Stain Remover. ("Tomato sauce? Red wine? The blood of six he-goats? Come, let us do laundry. Though thy sins be as scarlet, yet they will be white as snow—or thy money back!")

And Lenny showed Murray a financial summary of the results, with an abundance of graphs and tables. And Murray said, "This is fantastic!"

And he cheered up considerably.

So Murray and Lenny wound down their schedule. And they packed their belongings and set off.

And they journeyed through the lands of the Amorites, the Jebusites, the Edomites, the Socialites, and the Transvestites. They visited Babylon, Jericho, and Great Neck. Then they took the Belt Parkway south and continued until they reached Boca Raton.

chapter xviii

The Golden Years

And Boca was a bright and cheerful land, a place of well-tended lawns dotted with houses, and pleasant paths humming with golf carts. And there were pools and springs and lakes in abundance, most of them man-made. For the people who dwelt there felt that, though the Lord watereth the earth, sometimes He putteth the water in the wrong place.

And when they were settled there, each day Murray devoted himself to fasting and atonement, beginning right after breakfast, with a break for lunch. And these were the other activities of Murray which he did every day: nonimpact aerobics, having his blood pressure checked, napping, and golf with Lenny, followed by dinner at four P.M. at the Finicky Flounder. And in the evenings from time to time he played cards or went line dancing.

And it happened that when Murray was golfing, he was sometimes recognized on the fairways and greens. And the people prostrated themselves before him and beseeched him for guidance. And although he was retired, yet he answered them.

Some would ask, "Whence cometh wisdom?"

And he would say unto them, "Fear the Lord. Therein lies wisdom."

And others would ask, "Where dwelleth understanding?"

And he would say unto them, "Forsake evil. Therein lies understanding."

And still others would ask, "How can I get more distance on my tee shots?"

And he would say unto them, "Square thy

shoulders, bend at the waist, and transfer power from thy torso. Therein lies a tee shot."

And these were the years of Murray's life which he lived: they were three hundred and twenty. Though sometimes Murray told attractive widows that the years of his life were only two hundred and ninety, for he thought it would make a better impression.

But to Lenny, Murray moaned, "I am an old man, in a good old age, and full of years. Yea, verily, my mind is going. My early two-hundreds are a complete blur. Soon, you will have to bury me in the burial place of the buried.

"For it will be my time to give up the ghost and be taken away from thee. To lie down and rise not. To be gathered unto my people. To let my gray head go down to my grave. To go the way of all the earth. To pass over the river Jordan. To retire to the ultimate seniors community. To play pinochle with the angels. To shout

David M. Bader

'Fore!' to my forefathers. To do aquacise with my ancestors. To——"

And Lenny said, "Yea, verily, I know. You've been saying that for the last century."

But Murray continued, "Lenny, thou must be my successor and carry on. Here, takest thou my mantle."

And Lenny said, "It's a bit big for me."

And Murray answered, "You can have it altered."

And Lenny said, "What are these stains?"

Then Murray gave Lenny his blessing, saying, "May those who curse thee be cursed but blessed be those that bless thee. And cursed be those that bless those that curse thee, and also cursed be those who curse those who curse those who bless those that curse thee. But blessed be those who curse those that bless those who curse those that bless thee."

Whereupon a great pillar of clouds suddenly came down from the heavens and enveloped Murray. And the Lord was in the pillar. And He spoke directly to Murray, God to man, deity to prophet, omnipotent Ruler of the Universe to active senior.

And the Lord said, "Murray! It's good to see you again so soon."

And Murray asked, "So soon? Where hast thou been? From the rising of the sun to its setting I have called to Thee aloud. Thy statutes have been my songs, yea, literally, and not just in the shower. Which may be the reason people sometimes avoid me. Yet thou appearest not. I was beginning to think thou wouldst never show."

And the Lord said unto him, "Son of Irving, a thousand years in my sight are but a day that is past. I hope you haven't been waiting long."

Then the Lord looked upon Murray and

saw that Murray had waxed old and stricken in years.

And the Lord said, "Murray, thou hast waxed old and stricken in years!"

And Murray said unto the Lord, "Thanks for mentioning it."

Then Murray unburdened himself of the questions that had vexed him over the years:

>Why the floods, plagues, and pestilence—
>canst thou think of no other way to get
>our attention?

>Why do the righteous suffer while the
>wicked prosper?

>Are the meek really rewarded in the end,
>or is it all just about whom you know?

>Why am I charged for missing a doctor's
>appointment yet not compensated when
>I spend hours in the waiting room?

Why are we not supposed to speak thy name out loud? Not that we could if we wanted to. YHWH. Is that a text message?

If man is created in thine image, why am I not invisible? Where are my super-powers?

Why do my dental fillings fall out only when I'm traveling?

Is there an afterlife? If so, what about after that?

Why do the nations rage?

What are all those surcharges on my phone bill?

Why do so many Jews go into advertising?

Why isn't lobster kosher instead of gefilte fish?

Then the Lord answered Murray. And He revealed the future of mankind, explained the purpose of human suffering, and described the afterlife in detail. Though with respect to why Murray was not invisible and the reason so many Jews go into advertising, He told Murray he would have to look into those and get back to him. Then He departed, promising to be in touch again soon.

chapter six

THE DEATH OF MURRAY

And when the Lord had left and the pillar of clouds had lifted, Murray said unto Lenny, "I have heard the voice of the Lord and have had a great vision. Yea verily, He hath kept his promise to me."

And Lenny said, "His timing certainly leaveth something to be desired."

But Murray continued, "He hath dealt bountifully with me. I must sing Him a new song. Where is my harp?"

For Murray had taken up the instrument in retirement, and he was entirely self-taught. And Lenny had hidden the harp to preserve his own sanity and to avoid upsetting the neighbors and their pets.

Wherefore Murray proceeded without it, singing:

> *I will give thanks unto the Lord.*
> *For He forsaketh not his faithful.*
> *I waited patiently, and he heard my cry.*
> *He hath put a new song in my mouth.*
> *Not the catchiest, but it hath its moments.*
> *How excellent is His name!*
> *"God"—short, sweet, and to the point,*
> *not like "Quetzalcoatl" or "Huitzilopochtli,"*
> *yet somehow more serious than "Biff" or*
>   *"Trey."*
> *How great are his works!*
> *The heavens have proclaimed His glory.*
> *The skies have declared His handiwork,*
> *or perhaps that was skywriting.*
> *All the same, it was impressive.*
> *He hath revealed the deep and secret things.*
> *He knoweth what is in the darkness.*

For if he knoweth not, who would?
He hath spoken and explained everything,
about this world and the next,
except for a few things, like
why I am not invisible and
why so many Jews go into advertising.
Yea, verily, He is my strength and song,
even if His timing leaveth something to be
desired.
Though He slay me, yet will I trust in Him,
probably not in that order, however.
For His word is a lamp unto my feet
and a light unto my path.

And Murray said to Lenny, "I hope you are getting all of this down."

Then he recounted to Lenny all that the Almighty had revealed to him.

And Lenny tried to interrupt, but Murray would not be stopped. And when he finally paused for a breath, Lenny said, "Hold on a second. This pen isn't working. Let's back up. What came after 'lamp'?"

But at that moment there descended from the sky a chariot of fire with thundering horses, and in a whirlwind Murray was borne aloft.

And Lenny watched the fiery chariot climb toward the heavens with Murray on board, talking and gesticulating. For Murray was not only a chosen prophet of the Lord but also a notorious backseat driver.

Then it vanished from view.

So Lenny took up the mantle of Murray and went in search of a dry cleaner.

chapter xx

THE RETURN OF MURRAY

And it came to pass that Loofah was looking for a stray goat and had sneaked onto the grounds of a posh country club in search of it, when she heard a loud splash.

And when she looked about, she spied the burning wreck of a chariot that had landed nearby in a water hazard. Emerging from it was Murray, alive, but wet and shaken, with his clothing scorched and in tatters.

And Loofah helped him dry off and gave him new garments, woven entirely of goat hair. And though they were a bit scratchy, still the Bermuda shorts, shirt, and socks all matched and were very sharp.

And Lenny arrived shortly after, having seen the crash from a distance. And Murray asked Lenny, "Why art thou holding my mantle?"

For he remembered nothing of what had happened.

And Lenny explained, "You had a vision, and you were about to tell me about it when a chariot drove by and scooped you up and climbed into the sky. It was on fire. Literally burning. Everything in flames, even the wheels. It didn't take a prophet to predict that something bad was going to happen. You're lucky to be alive."

And while Murray took in these things, Lenny asked, "Was the driver drunk? Was there a chariot design flaw? Because either way, I think we may have a lawsuit."

And Murray could not say, but he agreed to consult an attorney.

And when he was fully rested, he took back

his mantle. And Lenny picked up his writer's inkhorn, and Loofah rounded up her goats.

Then they hastened off the grounds of the country club, for none of them was a member there. And it was four-thirty P.M. and they were late for dinner.

acknowledgments

This edition of *The Book of Murray* would not have been possible without the help of experts in a number of fields, including Near Eastern languages, archaeology, and religious history. These brilliant scholars cannot be named here, however, as each one pleaded not to be mentioned. Such modesty is rare and truly inspiring.

The editor is also deeply grateful to Kate Kennedy at Harmony Books, literary agent John Boswell, and kibbitzing attorney-at-law Benjamin E. Rosenberg, Esq., for their indispensable comments and suggestions. As always, he is grateful to his parents, whose constant noodging led, however unintentionally, to many new insights.

Acknowledgments

With respect to *The Book of Murray*, he takes full responsibility for the typos. All substantive problems are the fault of others, namely the Prophet Murray.

About David M. Bader

A native New Yorker, David M. Bader is the author of several books, including *Haikus for Jews: For You, a Little Wisdom* and *Zen Judaism: For You, a Little Enlightenment.* He began work on this book after an image of the Prophet Murray appeared to him on a toasted bagel.